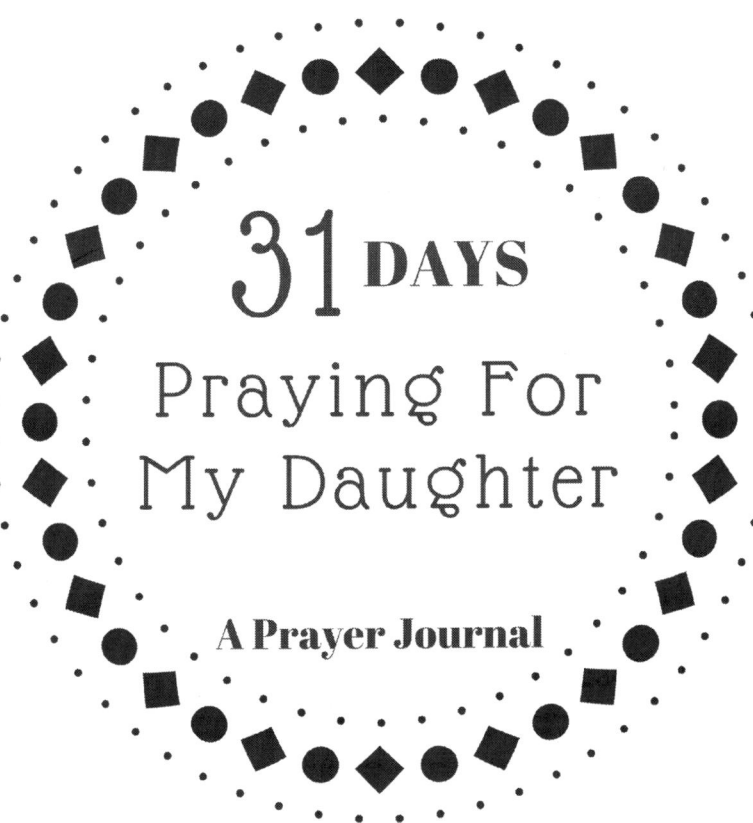

Susan K Macias

Copyright

31 Days: Praying For My Daughter; A Prayer Journal
Susan K. Macias

Copyright © 2018 by Susan Macias. All rights reserved. Reproduction of this publication in whole or part without express written consent is strictly prohibited.

ISBN 978 0 9993085 2 3

Unless otherwise noted, Scripture quotations are from the English Standard Version® (ESV®) (The Holy Bible, English Standard Version®), copyright © 2001 by Crossway, a publishing ministry of Good News Publishers. Used by permission. All rights reserved.

With all my heart
I dedicate this book
to my daughters and my
daughters-in-love.

I promise to
never stop praying.

Rejoice always,

pray without ceasing,

give thanks in all circumstances;

for this is the will of God in Christ Jesus for you.

1 Thessalonians 5:16-18

Table of Contents

Instructions		7
Daughter Questionnaire		11
Day 1:	My Attitude	13
Days 2 – 5:	Her Faith	19
Days 6 – 9:	Her Identity	37
Days 10 – 13:	Her Value	55
Days 14 – 17:	Her Heart	73
Days 18 – 21:	Her Relationships	91
Days 22 – 25:	Her Personality	109
Days 26 – 29:	Her Path	127
Day 30:	My Thankfulness	145
Day 31:	Keep Praying	151
Resources		157

31 DAYS
Praying For My Daughter

Welcome Prayer Warrior Mom!

How this journal works:

- **Day 1**: You will start this prayer journey praying for your own attitude, because sometimes our Mama attitudes stink. Trust me on this. I know. Don't ask me how I know, but I can attest to the need for prayer in this area. The goal of Day 1 is to shift your reliance from yourself to the Lord, the only One who can truly affect change.
- **Days 2 – 29**: These days are divided into seven sections, each four days long. These sections focus on different, specific areas of your girl's life.
- **Day 30**: Every previous Day you will have recorded one item you are thankful for in your daughter's life in the Day 30 section. Day 30 will be thanking the Lord for each of these things.
- **Day 31**: Don't skip this day- it wraps up the journal and sends you off on your continued prayer journey.

Each Day is formatted the same. There is a short instruction, followed by a Scripture from which that day's prayer is taken. You will notice the bolded areas which will show you where each of the following six prayer points are drawn from.

Each prayer has space to journal your thoughts, or you could use the space to write down the date when you prayed this. Don't forget to go back and record answers as you see them.

Following that are some thought questions with room for you to journal.

Just a few more thoughts:

- I am proud of and grateful for you. Today's daughters need prayer covering. Yay you! You are blessing your girl.
- Whenever I pray for my daughter I realize the same issues in my own life could use a bit of prayer. That is a good thing! I am not hypocritical if I pray for an area my daughter struggles with, where I do as well. It just gives me better understanding of her needs.
- There is lots of writing space in this journal. Please use it in ways that aide you best.
- Implement the 31 Days in full freedom. You can do 31 days in a row, or you can just go through it as you can until all 31 Days are prayed through. You could pray through one section a week for seven weeks. Or, pick it up when you remember and start up where you left off.
- Don't listen to the enemy's accusations that you aren't doing it right. There is no right way and as long as you keep coming back and praying, you are fighting the fight for your daughter.
- The 31 Days do not have to be in a row for the cumulative effect of concentrated prayer to add up.
- Use this journal over and over. You could choose a different color of ink each time through.
- There is a place to jot down prayer requests in the Resources, as well as more daughter questionnaires if you need them.

One more thing: Don't be discouraged.

- You haven't messed up too much.
- You haven't dropped too many balls.
- You haven't ruined your daughter.
- Your daughter hasn't sinned too badly.
- Your daughter hasn't wandered too far.
- Your daughter's heart is not past the healing of Jesus.

You have a powerful weapon to fight for your girl, and it is not this journal. The purpose of this book is simply to help you use the weapon effectively.

You are armed with prayer and the Word of God. Praying God's Word is a weapon the enemy can't stand against.

Don't grow weary. Don't stop. Don't let a failure keep you from starting over. Just keep coming back over and over to prayer. The Lord is waiting for you with open arms, to listen and to act.

Never forget your Heavenly Father's promise:

> to grant to those who mourn in Zion-- to give them a beautiful headdress instead of ashes, the oil of gladness instead of mourning, the garment of praise instead of a faint spirit; that they may be called oaks of righteousness, the planting of the LORD, that he may be glorified. (Isaiah 61:3 ESV)

Before you get started, fill out the following Daughter Questionnaire. It will help you think through the unique ways the Lord has designed your daughter and will help you pray effectively for her.

If you have more than one daughter, or want to come back later and fill this out again as your daughter grows and changes, there are more copies in the Resources section.

Daughter Questionnaire

Daughter's name: _____
_____

Describe your daughter's relationship with the Lord:
_____
_____
_____
_____

Describe your daughter's personality:
_____
_____
_____
_____

What are the biggest challenges facing your daughter:
_____
_____
_____
_____

What are your daughter's greatest strengths:
_____
_____
_____
_____

My Attitude

DAY 1

One of the biggest hurdles of an effective prayer life can be my own attitude. How about you? Begin this 31 Days of prayer for your daughter by praying for your own heart and demeanor. Faith and hope on the inside can't help but show up on our outside!

> ~ For this reason **I bow my knees before the Father**, from whom **every family in heaven and on earth is named**, that according to the riches of his glory **he may grant you to be strengthened** with power **through his Spirit in your inner being** (Ephesians 3:14-16)
>
> ~ **I thank God whom I serve**, as did my ancestors, with a clear conscience, as **I remember you constantly in my prayers** night and day. (Timothy 1:3)

Father, I bow to You and commit the next 31 days of prayer to You.

_____
_____
_____
_____

Lord, thank You for forming, establishing, and naming our family.

_____
_____
_____
_____

DAY 1
My Attitude

Jesus, please give me the strength I need to not only pray, but to WANT to pray.

_____
_____
_____
_____

Please use Your Spirit to work on my inner heart so that I can serve my daughter in prayer joyfully.

_____
_____
_____
_____

Lord Jesus, I pledge to serve You only – not my dreams, not my expectations, not my desires. Only You.

_____
_____
_____
_____

I ask You, Lord, give me the strength to constantly pray for my daughter. Help me pray instead of nagging, prodding, worrying, fretting, or grieving.

_____
_____
_____
_____

DAY 1
My Attitude

In what areas is prayer a struggle for me?

_____
_____
_____
_____
_____
_____
_____
_____
_____

What burdens am I carrying about my daughter that weigh down my heart? After writing down the answer, take a moment to give these to Jesus.

_____
_____
_____
_____
_____
_____
_____
_____

DAY 1
My Attitude

PRAY through today's Scripture. Use the space below to write a specific prayer for your attitude about praying for your daughter for the next 30 days.

_____
_____
_____
_____
_____
_____
_____
_____

WRITE one item of thankfulness about your daughter on Day 30. (Turn to page 147 and record your thought on Day 1. You will repeat this on each day of prayer.)

Notes, thoughts, praise...

_____
_____
_____
_____
_____
_____
_____
_____

Faith

DAY 2

You will pray for your daughter's faith for the next four days. If she is a believer already, then this is for a deepening, vibrant faith. If she is not yet a believer, then you are praying for her to personally put all her trust and hope in Jesus. He is the only One worthy of our faith and no matter where your daughter is on her faith journey, you can pray for that relationship.

> Jesus said to her, "**I am the resurrection and the life**. Whoever believes in me, though he die, **yet shall he live**, and **everyone who lives and believes** in me shall never die. Do you believe this?" She said to him, "**Yes, Lord; I believe** that **you are the Christ**, the Son of God, **who is coming** into the world." (John 11:25-27)

Lord, I ask that:

~ my daughter's faith would rest in You, the resurrected Jesus.

_____
_____
_____
_____

~ my daughter would experience new and renewed life through faith in You.

_____
_____
_____
_____

DAY 2
Faith

~ my daughter would believe in Jesus ONLY for salvation.

_____
_____
_____
_____

~ Lord, please call my daughter to Yourself, that she would look at You and say, "Yes! I believe."

_____
_____
_____
_____

~ that You would be the one and only Lord in her life.

_____
_____
_____
_____

~ she would have faith that You are alive and coming again.

_____
_____
_____
_____

DAY 2
Faith

In what areas is faith a strength for my daughter?

_____
_____
_____
_____
_____
_____
_____
_____

What burdens am I carrying about my daughter's faith that I need to give back to Jesus?

_____
_____
_____
_____
_____
_____
_____
_____

DAY 2
Faith

PRAY through today's Scripture. Use the space below to write a specific prayer for your daughter.

_____
_____
_____
_____
_____
_____
_____
_____

WRITE one item of thankfulness about your daughter on Day 30.

Notes, thoughts, praise...

_____
_____
_____
_____
_____
_____
_____
_____

Faith

DAY 3

Part of praying for your daughter's faith requires you to have enough faith to be patient while God works in her. How precious that He gives you the job of praying during the process. You pray, He works. Rest in Jesus, dear one, as He works in your daughter. Trust Him.

> To them **God chose to make known** how great among the Gentiles are the **riches of the glory of this mystery**, which is **Christ in you**, the **hope of glory**. Him we proclaim, warning everyone and **teaching everyone with all wisdom**, that we may present everyone **mature in Christ. For this I toil**, struggling with all his energy that he powerfully works within me. (Colossians 1:27-29)

Lord Jesus, I ask that You would:

~ make Yourself known in a deep and personal way to my daughter.

_____
_____
_____
_____

~ cause my daughter's faith to draw from the richness of Jesus in her.

_____
_____
_____
_____

DAY 3
Faith

~ make my daughter's faith rest in nothing but You and Your life in her.

_____
_____
_____
_____

~ richly grow glorious hope in her heart.

_____
_____
_____
_____

~ cause my daughter to grow more and more mature daily as she experiences You.

_____
_____
_____
_____

~ please give me wisdom and energy to be an example of faith in You that I might teach my daughter how valuable my faith in You is to me.

_____
_____
_____
_____

DAY 3
Faith

How is faith a challenge for my daughter?

_____
_____
_____
_____
_____
_____
_____
_____
_____

How can I praise my daughter about her faith today? (If nothing specific comes to mind then don't forget to ask the Lord for help with an idea.)

_____
_____
_____
_____
_____
_____
_____
_____
_____

DAY 3
Faith

PRAY through today's Scripture. Use the space below to write a specific prayer for your daughter.

WRITE one item of thankfulness about your daughter on Day 30.

Notes, thoughts, praise...

Faith

DAY 4

What care we receive from our Heavenly Father as He rescues, protects, and holds us, and then provides us a safe place to land. Today, pray for your daughter to have faith that He will care for her.

> He said, "**The LORD is my rock and my fortress and my deliverer**, my God, my rock, in whom I take refuge, my shield, and the horn of my salvation, **my stronghold and my refuge, my savior**; you save me from violence. ... "He sent from on high, **he took me; he drew me out** of many waters. **He rescued me from my strong enemy**, from those who hated me, for they were too mighty for me. ... **He brought me out into a broad place**; he rescued me, because **he delighted in me**. (2 Samuel 22:2-3, 17-18, 20)

Lord, I pray that:

~ my daughter's faith would be as solid as You, and she would experience You as her rock, her fortress, and her deliverer.

_____
_____
_____
_____

~ her faith would would rest in You, her stronghold, her refuge, and her Savior.

_____
_____
_____
_____

DAY 4
Faith

~ please draw her away from the world and closer to You.

~ her faith would would be in You to defeat her enemy and to rescue her.

~ You would bring her to a broad, secure faith.

~ my daughter would experience delight in You.

DAY 4
Faith

Where do I see my daughter struggling with her faith?

_____
_____
_____
_____
_____
_____
_____
_____
_____
_____

What is something I can do with or for my daughter to encourage her faith? How can I demonstrate my love for her, no matter where she is right now?

_____
_____
_____
_____
_____
_____
_____
_____
_____
_____

DAY 4
Faith

PRAY through today's Scripture. Use the space below to write a specific prayer for your daughter.

WRITE one item of thankfulness about your daughter on Day 30.

Notes, thoughts, praise...

Faith

DAY 5

Today you will ask the Holy Spirit to work faith deep into your daughter's heart. All true spiritual work is done by the Spirit and can protect believers from getting tripped up by a works-based faith. I want my girls to rest in His work for them, not in what they do.

> But when the **goodness and loving kindness of God our Savior** appeared, **he saved us**, **not because of works done by us in righteousness**, but according to his own mercy, by the **washing of regeneration and renewal of the Holy Spirit**, whom **he poured out on us richly through Jesus Christ** our Savior, so that being **justified by his grace** we might become **heirs according to the hope of eternal life**. (Titus 3:4-7)

My Jesus, I ask You that:

~ my daughter's faith thrive as it rests in Your goodness and loving kindness.

___

___

___

___

~ my daughter's assurance would rest in You only and not in any of her works that she does for You.

___

___

___

___

DAY 5
Faith

~ my daughter's faith would grow through the Holy Spirit which washes and renews her, and brings new life.

_____
_____
_____
_____

~ You would richly pour out Your Holy Spirit on my daughter.

_____
_____
_____
_____

~ she would look to nothing but Your grace for justification.

_____
_____
_____
_____

~ her faith would give her assurance and hope of her eternal life with You and her inheritance as Your heir.

_____
_____
_____
_____

DAY 5
Faith

When do I see my daughter have victory with faith?

_____
_____
_____
_____
_____
_____
_____
_____
_____

What specific needs have been revealed after praying for my daughter's faith for four days?

_____
_____
_____
_____
_____
_____
_____
_____
_____

DAY 5
Faith

PRAY through today's Scripture. Use the space below to write a specific prayer for your daughter.

_____
_____
_____
_____
_____
_____
_____
_____

WRITE one item of thankfulness about your daughter on Day 30.

Notes, thoughts, praise...

_____
_____
_____
_____
_____
_____
_____
_____

Identity

Identity

DAY 6

In today's world our girl's identity is under attack. For the next four days you are going to fight back and pray for your daughter's identity to be founded squarely on and in Jesus.

> For **you formed** my inward parts; **you knitted me together** in my mother's womb. I praise you, for **I am fearfully and wonderfully made**. Wonderful are your works; my soul knows it very well. **My frame was not hidden from you,** when I was being made in secret, intricately woven in the depths of the earth. **Your eyes saw my unformed substance**; in your book were **written, every one of them, the days that were formed for me**, when as yet there was none of them. How **precious to me are your thoughts, O God**! How vast is the sum of them! (Psalm 139:13-17)

Dear Jesus, I pray today that:

~ my daughter would find her identity in being designed and formed by You purposefully, exactly as she is.

_____
_____
_____
_____

~ she would find her identity in being Your special creation for Your purposes

_____
_____
_____
_____

DAY 6
Identity

~ my daughter would be secure in knowing she is always seen by You.

_____
_____
_____
_____

~ she would confidently believe that You have seen and planned her, even before her conception, for Your glory.

_____
_____
_____
_____

~ she would rest in the knowledge that You have planned her days, and please help her rest in Your plan for her life.

_____
_____
_____
_____

~ Your precious thoughts toward her would be more important than any other person so that her identity can rest in her relationship with You.

_____
_____
_____
_____

DAY 6
Identity

In what areas is my daughter's identity secure?

_____
_____
_____
_____
_____
_____
_____
_____
_____

What burdens am I carrying about my daughter's identity that I need to give back to Jesus?

_____
_____
_____
_____
_____
_____
_____
_____
_____

DAY 6
Identity

PRAY through today's Scripture. Use the space below to write a specific prayer for your daughter.

_____
_____
_____
_____
_____
_____
_____
_____

WRITE one item of thankfulness about your daughter on Day 30.

Notes, thoughts, praise...

_____
_____
_____
_____
_____
_____
_____
_____

Identity

DAY 7

Lack of contentment with current circumstances can really do a number on your daughter's peace with who God created her to be, and where He has placed her. Pray today for the peaceful attitude that will allow her to rest her identity in Jesus.

> Trust in the LORD, and do good; **dwell in the land and befriend faithfulness. Delight yourself in the LORD, and he will give you the desires of your heart. Commit your way to the LORD; trust in him**, and he will act. ... **Be still before the LORD and wait patiently** for him; **fret not yourself over the one who prospers in his way**, over the man who carries out evil devices! **Refrain from anger, and forsake wrath**! Fret not yourself; it tends only to evil. (Psalm 37:3-5, 7-8)

Dear Jesus, please:

~ help my daughter dwell peacefully where she is, content where You have her so that she doesn't try to find her identity elsewhere.

~ help her find her delight in You and please form her desires that they would glorify You and build Your kingdom.

DAY 7
Identity

~ lead her to totally commit her way and her identity to You, trusting You to lead her where she should go.

_____
_____
_____
_____

~ bring a peace to my daughter so that she would be willing to be still before You, waiting on You to move in her life.

_____
_____
_____
_____

~ help my daughter to not fret about other people or be drawn to those who seem to succeed while doing the wrong thing.

_____
_____
_____
_____

~ keep my daughter from anger against either those who love her or those who oppose her.

_____
_____
_____
_____

DAY 7
Faith

How is her identity a challenge for my daughter?

_____
_____
_____
_____
_____
_____
_____
_____
_____

How can I praise my daughter about where she places her identity today? (If nothing specific comes to mind then don't forget to ask the Lord for help with an idea.)

_____
_____
_____
_____
_____
_____
_____
_____
_____

DAY 7
Identity

PRAY through today's Scripture. Use the space below to write a specific prayer for your daughter.

WRITE one item of thankfulness about your daughter on Day 30.

Notes, thoughts, praise...

Identity

DAY 8

What a gift we have to find our identity in Christ, who not only died for us, but also lives in us, His people! Pray today for that life to be a place of great freedom and joy for your girl.

> I have been **crucified with Christ**. It is **no longer I who live**, but **Christ who lives in me**. And the **life I now live** in the flesh **I live by faith** in the Son of God, who **loved me and gave himself for me**. (Galatians 2:20)

Jesus, I pray that:

~ my daughter would live in the freedom and forgiveness found in identifying with Your crucifixion.

_____
_____
_____
_____

~ my daughter would be released from the bondage of hanging onto her life for herself.

_____
_____
_____
_____

DAY 8
Identity

~ she would live with all the fullness You bring to her.

_____
_____
_____
_____

~ her life would be wholly and unreservedly Yours so she would be able to find her identity in You.

_____
_____
_____
_____

~ my daughter's faith would rest in You and Your finished work on the cross.

_____
_____
_____
_____

~ she would feel, know, and rest in Your completed love so much that she would not need the approval of any other person.

_____
_____
_____
_____

DAY 8
Identity

Where do I see my daughter struggling with her identity?

_____
_____
_____
_____
_____
_____
_____
_____
_____

What is something I can do with or for my daughter to encourage her to find her identity in Jesus? How can I demonstrate my love for her, no matter where she is right now?

_____
_____
_____
_____
_____
_____
_____
_____
_____

DAY 8
Identity

PRAY through today's Scripture. Use the space below to write a specific prayer for your daughter.

WRITE one item of thankfulness about your daughter on Day 30.

Notes, thoughts, praise...

Identity

DAY 9

There are so many counterfeit places to find identity. Today, pray that your daughter would discover the great joy of her identity being cemented in Jesus. There is nowhere else that will bring life and hope to her heart.

> I will **greatly rejoice in the LORD; my soul shall exult in my God**, for **he has clothed me with the garments of salvation; he has covered me with the robe of righteousness**, as a **bridegroom** decks himself like a priest with a beautiful headdress, and as a **bride** adorns herself with her jewels. (Isaiah 61:10)

Lord, I ask that You would:

~ cause great joy to fill my daughter's heart through her relationship with You.

_____
_____
_____
_____

~ fill my daughter's soul with Your presence that she would overflow with praise.

_____
_____
_____
_____

DAY 9
Identity

~ clothe my daughter with Your salvation so completely that she would not need to find her identity in what she wears.

_____
_____
_____
_____

~ cover my daughter with Your righteousness so completely that she would never try to find her identity in what she does.

_____
_____
_____
_____

~ fulfill her need for love as her "bridegroom" so much that she never tries to find her identity through a romantic relationship.

_____
_____
_____
_____

~ assure her of her relationship with You as "bride" so much that she would wear the identity of "dearly loved" and rest in that security.

_____
_____
_____
_____

DAY 9
Identity

Where do I see my daughter have victory with identity?

_____
_____
_____
_____
_____
_____
_____
_____
_____

What specific needs have been revealed after praying for my daughter's identity for four days?

_____
_____
_____
_____
_____
_____
_____
_____
_____

DAY 9
Identity

PRAY through today's Scripture. Use the space below to write a specific prayer for your daughter.

_____
_____
_____
_____
_____
_____
_____
_____

WRITE one item of thankfulness about your daughter on Day 30.

Notes, thoughts, praise…

_____
_____
_____
_____
_____
_____
_____
_____

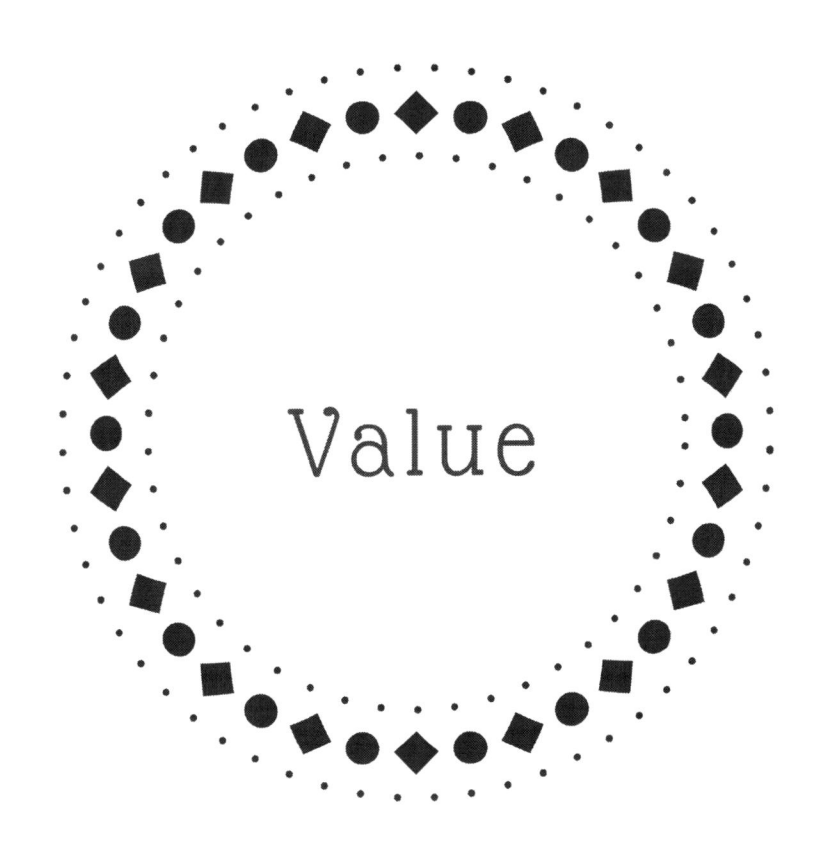

Value

Value

DAY 10

We are highly valued by the Lord. But the world wants our girls to think their value rests in what they achieve or what they look like. For the next four days pray that your daughter gains an understanding of how highly valuable she truly is in God's eyes.

> **Know that the LORD**, he is God! It is **he who made us**, and **we are his; we are his people**, and the **sheep of his pasture**. Enter his gates with thanksgiving, and his courts with praise! **Give thanks to him**; bless his name! For the LORD is good; **his steadfast love endures forever**, and his faithfulness to all generations. (Psalm 100:3-5)

Jesus, I ask You to:

~ help my daughter realize her value as Your child.

_____
_____
_____
_____

~ please remove the lie that she is only a product of chance, and confirm that she is made, created, formed, and on purpose.

_____
_____
_____
_____

DAY 10
Value

~ help my daughter to realize her value in being YOURS. If she does not believe in You yet, please draw her heart into Your loving embrace.

_____
_____
_____
_____

~ help my daughter see the privilege of being under You as a Shepherd, that she would obey and follow You as she rests in belonging to You.

_____
_____
_____
_____

~ please grow thanksgiving in my daughter's heart as she realizes her value to You.

_____
_____
_____
_____

~ assure my daughter's heart of the reliability and permanence of Your love, which stands fast always.

_____
_____
_____
_____

DAY 10
Value

In what areas does my daughter find her value in the Lord?

___

What burdens am I carrying about my daughter's understanding of her value that I need to give back to Jesus?

___

DAY 10
Value

PRAY through today's Scripture. Use the space below to write a specific prayer for your daughter.

WRITE one item of thankfulness about your daughter on Day 30.

Notes, thoughts, praise...

Value

DAY 11

The world screams at our girls that sex is glamorous and is the way they can find value and love. Pray today that your daughter would see sex through God's eyes and believe His plan for the how, where, and when of it. And that she would see His restrictions as a confirmation of her great value.

> But he who is **joined to the Lord** becomes one spirit with him. **Flee from sexual immorality**. Every other sin a person commits is outside the body, but the sexually immoral person sins against his own body. Or do you not know that **your body is a temple of the Holy Spirit** within you, whom you have from God? **You are not your own**, for **you were bought with a price**. So **glorify God in your body**. (1 Corinthians 6:17-20)

Please help my daughter to:

~ see her value and sacredness as a young woman joined to You.

_____
_____
_____
_____

~ flee the sexual sin that the world promotes so heavily around her. Help her see that her value to You is worth so much more.

_____
_____
_____
_____

DAY 11
Value

~ understand the value of her physical body to You and that she can protect that through the power of Your Spirit.

_____
_____
_____
_____

~ see herself as Yours: belonging to You, valued by You, obligated to You, and set apart by You.

_____
_____
_____
_____

~ realize her extreme value in that she was worth You dying for. Please help her understand that the high price reflects her high value.

_____
_____
_____
_____

~ see the privilege of glorifying You in her body as a sign of her value.

_____
_____
_____
_____

DAY 11
Value

When is it a challenge for my daughter to see her value?

How can I praise my daughter about where she finds her value today? (If nothing specific comes to mind then don't forget to ask the Lord for help with an idea.)

DAY 11
Value

PRAY through today's Scripture. Use the space below to write a specific prayer for your daughter.

WRITE one item of thankfulness about your daughter on Day 30.

Notes, thoughts, praise...

Value

DAY 12

Pray today that your daughter would understand her value by realizing all that the Lord has provided for her. His great love, care, and provision for her are proof of her worth.

> **Strength and dignity are her clothing**, and she **laughs at the time to come**. (Proverbs 31:25)
>
> **Light is sown for the righteous**, and **joy for the upright in heart**. (Psalm 97:11)
>
> the LORD appeared to him from far away. **I have loved you with an everlasting love**; therefore **I have continued my faithfulness to you**. (Jeremiah 31:3)

Lord Jesus, I ask You to:

~ give my daughter the understanding that she is more than what she wears, and help her put on Your dignity.

_____
_____
_____
_____

~ help my daughter understand her value to You so well that she laughs at the future, no matter what is ahead.

_____
_____
_____
_____

DAY 12
Value

~ assist my daughter to see the light and truth You provide for her.

~ help her understand her value to You and see the evidence through all You provide for her - like joy for her heart.

~ give my girl a realization of Your lasting-forever love for her, and help her feel how valuable that makes her.

~ help my daughter understand that her continued value does not depend on her but on Your faithfulness, which never stops.

DAY 12
Value

What areas of my daughter's life make her question her value?

_____
_____
_____
_____
_____
_____
_____
_____
_____
_____

What is something I can do with or for my daughter to encourage her to find her value in Jesus? How can I demonstrate my love for her, no matter where she is right now?

_____
_____
_____
_____
_____
_____
_____
_____
_____
_____

DAY 12
Value

PRAY through today's Scripture. Use the space below to write a specific prayer for your daughter.

_____
_____
_____
_____
_____
_____
_____
_____

WRITE one item of thankfulness about your daughter on Day 30.

Notes, thoughts, praise...

_____
_____
_____
_____
_____
_____
_____
_____

Value

DAY 13

God's gifts and His work in our lives demonstrate how much He values us. Pray for your daughter's understanding so that she can grasp the deep meaning of all the Lord's work in her life.

> For **by grace you have been saved** through faith. And this is **not your own doing; it is the gift of God, not a result of works**, so that no one may boast. For **we are his workmanship**, created in Christ Jesus for good works, which God prepared beforehand, that **we should walk in them**. ... So then you are no longer strangers and aliens, but **you are fellow citizens** with the saints and members of the household of God, ... In him you also are being **built together into a dwelling place for God** by the Spirit. (Ephesians 2:8-10, 19, 22)

Jesus, please help my daughter see:

~ her salvation is wholly dependent on You.

_____
_____
_____
_____

~ she never needs to try and earn her relationship with You because it is Your gift, not her doing.

_____
_____
_____
_____

DAY 13
Value

~ her ultimate value is based upon Your workmanship in her life.

_____
_____
_____
_____

~ the value of the work You have given her to do and please help her walk in Your plan for her life.

_____
_____
_____
_____

~ her citizenship in Your Kingdom and that she need never feel like an alien or a stranger again.

_____
_____
_____
_____

~ her value is proved in that she can be Your dwelling place.

_____
_____
_____
_____

DAY 13
Value

Where does my daughter walk victoriously in understanding her value?

_____

What specific needs have been revealed after praying for my daughter's understanding of her value?

_____

DAY 13
Value

PRAY through today's Scripture. Use the space below to write a specific prayer for your daughter.

WRITE one item of thankfulness about your daughter on Day 30.

Notes, thoughts, praise...

Heart

Heart

DAY 14

You will be praying for your daughter's heart for the next four days. Her heart is where her hopes, loves, and fears reside. When her heart rests in the Lord and His plans for her, she can weather the storms of life with contentment and trust.

> Not that I am speaking of **being in need**, for I have learned in **whatever situation I am to be content**. **I know how to be brought low**, and **I know how to abound**. In any and every circumstance, **I have learned the secret of facing plenty and hunger**, abundance and need. **I can do all things through him who strengthens me**. (Philippians 4:11-13)

Dearest Jesus, I ask You to :

~ please always reveal to my daughter's heart that it needs You and nothing else.

_____
_____
_____
_____

~ help my daughter to be content where she is, and with what she has, not being jealous of others.

_____
_____
_____
_____

DAY 14
Heart

~ help my daughter in her areas of struggle, trusting You to work in and through them.

_____
_____
_____
_____

~ help my daughter in her strengths to be humble and to use them for Your glory.

_____
_____
_____
_____

~ assist my girl to face abundance and lack with her faith in You intact so that no matter what she has or doesn't have, her love for You would grow.

_____
_____
_____
_____

~ grow her understanding that she always can do everything she needs to through YOUR strength, not her own.

_____
_____
_____
_____

DAY 14
Heart

In what areas is my daughter's heart strong?

_____
_____
_____
_____
_____
_____
_____
_____
_____

What burdens am I carrying about my daughter's heart that I need to give back to Jesus?

_____
_____
_____
_____
_____
_____
_____
_____
_____

DAY 14
Heart

PRAY through today's Scripture. Use the space below to write a specific prayer for your daughter.

WRITE one item of thankfulness about your daughter on Day 30.

Notes, thoughts, praise...

Heart

DAY 15

So many desires call out to our girls' hearts. Pray for your daughter to desire Jesus more than any other thing so that her whole heart can belong to Him alone.

> **Do not love the world** or **the things in the world**. If anyone loves the world, the love of the Father is not in him. For all that is in the world--the **desires of the flesh** and the **desires of the eyes** and **pride of life**--is not from the Father but is from the world. And the world is passing away along with its desires, but **whoever does the will of God abides forever**. (1 John 2:15-17)

Lord, please help my daughter to:

~ not love any of the world's claims more than she loves You.

_____
_____
_____
_____

~ not love the things the world offers more than she loves You.

_____
_____
_____
_____

DAY 15
Heart

~ give You every desire of her flesh: boys, clothes, friends, or any other thing she would love more than You.

_____
_____
_____
_____

~ give You every desire of her eyes: money, things, jealousies, or any other thing she would desire over You.

_____
_____
_____
_____

~ give You every pride: achievements, opinions, awards, or any other thing she would prize above You.

_____
_____
_____
_____

~ place her heart in Your hands forever that You could protect and guide it to Your best.

_____
_____
_____
_____

DAY 15
Heart

How is the direction of her heart a challenge for my daughter?

_____
_____
_____
_____
_____
_____
_____
_____
_____
_____

How can I praise my daughter about the state of her heart today? (If nothing specific comes to mind then don't forget to ask the Lord for help with an idea.)

_____
_____
_____
_____
_____
_____
_____
_____
_____
_____

DAY 15
Heart

PRAY through today's Scripture. Use the space below to write a specific prayer for your daughter.

_____
_____
_____
_____
_____
_____
_____
_____

WRITE one item of thankfulness about your daughter on Day 30.

Notes, thoughts, praise...

_____
_____
_____
_____
_____
_____
_____
_____

Heart

DAY 16

Life can be hard and people can be cruel. Today, pray that as your daughter experiences difficulties she will find her relief and healing in the Lord. He cares for her broken heart.

> When the **righteous cry for help**, the **LORD hears** and **delivers them** out of all their troubles. The **LORD is near to the brokenhearted** and **saves the crushed in spirit**. Many are the **afflictions of the righteous, but the LORD delivers** him out of them all. (Psalm 34:17-19)

Lord Jesus, please help my daughter's heart:

~ to cry out to You when she has problems and needs help.

_____
_____
_____
_____

~ rest in the trust that You always hear her when she calls to You.

_____
_____
_____

DAY 16
Heart

~ know she can rely on You to deliver her from any trouble.

_____
_____
_____
_____

~ rest in Your nearness when she feels broken or sad.

_____
_____
_____
_____

~ be healed when she is crushed in spirit, and help her run to You to be saved.

_____
_____
_____
_____

~ remain faithful through all the problems and trials she will be faced with, and that she would always turn to You for deliverance.

_____
_____
_____
_____

DAY 16
Heart

Where do I see my daughter struggling with her heart?

_____
_____
_____
_____
_____
_____
_____
_____
_____

What is something I can do with or for my daughter to encourage her to give Jesus her whole heart? How can I demonstrate my love for her, no matter where she is right now?

_____
_____
_____
_____
_____
_____
_____
_____
_____

DAY 16
Heart

PRAY through today's Scripture. Use the space below to write a specific prayer for your daughter.

WRITE one item of thankfulness about your daughter on Day 30.

Notes, thoughts, praise...

Heart

DAY 17

All of our hearts long for something to fulfill them, and your daughter is the same. Pray that she will find her fulfillment in the Lord – the only true and satisfying One to meet all of her heart's deepest needs.

> ~ **Keep your heart** with all vigilance, for **from it flow the springs of life**. (Proverbs 4:23)
> ~Little children, **let us** not **love** in word or talk but in **deed and in truth**. (1 John 3:18)
> ~As a deer pants for flowing streams, so **pants my soul for you**, O God. **My soul thirsts for God**, for the living God… (Psalm 42:1-2a)
> ~For where your **treasure is, there your heart** will be also. (Matthew 6:21)

Dear Lord I ask You to:

~ keep my daughter's heart close to You and teach her how to keep her own heart safe and secure with You.

_____
_____
_____
_____

~ cause life to bubble up and flow out of my daughter's heart to those around her.

_____
_____
_____
_____

DAY 17
Heart

~ grow love in my daughter's heart that would overflow into what she says and what she does.

~ cause my daughter's heart to desire You more than anything else.

~ create a thirst for You in her heart that would not be satisfied by any other thing than You.

~ help my daughter treasure You more than anything the world would offer her.

DAY 17
Heart

In what areas of her heart do I see my daughter having victory?

_____
_____
_____
_____
_____
_____
_____
_____

What specific needs have been revealed after praying for my daughter's heart?

_____
_____
_____
_____
_____
_____
_____
_____

DAY 17
Heart

PRAY through today's Scripture. Use the space below to write a specific prayer for your daughter.

WRITE one item of thankfulness about your daughter on Day 30.

Notes, thoughts, praise…

Relationships

Relationships

DAY 18

The people surrounding your daughter greatly influence her, so you want to bring these relationships before the Lord. Today, pray for her contentment, joy, and acceptance of the family in which God has placed her.

> Unless the **LORD builds the house**, those who build it labor in vain. Unless the **LORD watches over the city**, the watchman stays awake in vain. ... Behold, **children are a heritage** from the LORD, the fruit of the womb a reward. Like **arrows in the hand of a warrior** are the children of one's youth. **Blessed** is the man who fills his quiver with them! He shall not be put to shame when he **speaks with his enemies in the gate**. (Psalm 127:1, 3-5)

Lord, I ask you to help my daughter

~ see that she is in the exact family You desire her to be.

_____
_____
_____
_____

~ feel secure in Your protection and guidance of our family.

_____
_____
_____
_____

DAY 18
Relationships

~ rest in her position as a gift to her family. Show us how to effectively act that way and help her to feel that way.

_____
_____
_____
_____

~ become sharpened to be an effective arrow for You. Please help me to prepare her to be launched at the right time.

_____
_____
_____
_____

~ perceive Your many blessings in the relationships You have allowed for her.

_____
_____
_____
_____

~ feel secure in our love so that she can grow to be the leader You desire her to be.

_____
_____
_____
_____

DAY 18
Relationships

What relationships are healthy and fruitful in my daughter's life?

_____
_____
_____
_____
_____
_____
_____
_____
_____
_____

What burdens am I carrying about my daughter's relationships that I need to give back to Jesus?

_____
_____
_____
_____
_____
_____
_____
_____
_____
_____

DAY 18
Relationships

PRAY through today's Scripture. Use the space below to write a specific prayer for your daughter.

WRITE one item of thankfulness about your daughter on Day 30.

Notes, thoughts, praise...

Relationships

DAY 19

Some people in your daughter's life will be difficult and cause conflict. Pray for her to find her peace and rescue in Jesus, and for her to trust His working through those challenges.

> "**He sent from on high**, he took me; **he drew me out** of many waters. **He rescued me** from my strong enemy, from **those who hated me**, for they were too mighty for me. ... **He brought me out into a broad place**; he rescued me, because **he delighted in me**. (2 Sam 22:17-18, 20)

Jesus, I ask You to:

~ send help to my daughter, from on high, whenever she has difficult friendships.

_____
_____
_____
_____

~ cause her to turn to You for rescue when she feels overwhelmed with relationships.

_____
_____
_____
_____

DAY 19
Relationships

~ rescue my daughter from difficult or unkind "friends."

~ show my daughter how Your love is enough when others are hateful, and please help me love her through those challenges.

~ help her see the security You give her in our family and help her rest in Your security.

~ allow my daughter to experience Your delight in her in a tangible way.

DAY 19
Relationships

What relationships are a challenge for my daughter?

_____
_____
_____
_____
_____
_____
_____
_____

How can I praise my daughter about the state of her relationships with family and friends today? (If nothing specific comes to mind then don't forget to ask the Lord for help with an idea.)

_____
_____
_____
_____
_____
_____
_____
_____

DAY 19
Relationships

PRAY through today's Scripture. Use the space below to write a specific prayer for your daughter.

WRITE one item of thankfulness about your daughter on Day 30.

Notes, thoughts, praise...

Relationships

DAY 20

Jesus is our most faithful friend. Pray that your daughter realizes she can go to Him with every challenge, no matter how big or small. Even when the people around her are difficult, pray she knows that she always has a safe place to run.

> When the **righteous cry for help, the LORD hears** and **delivers them out of all their troubles**. The **LORD is near to the brokenhearted** and **saves the crushed in spirit**. Many are the **afflictions of the righteous**, but the **LORD delivers** him out of them all. (Psalm 34:17-19)

Lord Jesus, I ask You to:

~ give my daughter confidence that You always hear when she cries to You for help with the people in her life

_____
_____
_____

~ deliver my daughter out of her relationship troubles and show her where she needs to change if necessary.

_____
_____
_____

DAY 20
Relationships

~ help her feel Your nearness when she is sad and brokenhearted.

~ please direct her heart to Your saving grace when she struggles with people, whether in our family or with friends.

~ aide my girl so she is not surprised by afflictions, but to see them as opportunities to spend more time with You.

~ help her recognize and then praise You for all the help You give her.

DAY 20
Relationships

Where do I see my daughter struggling with relationships?

_____
_____
_____
_____
_____
_____
_____
_____
_____

What is something I can do with or for my daughter to encourage her in how she relates to the people in her life? How can I demonstrate my love for her, no matter where she is right now?

_____
_____
_____
_____
_____
_____
_____
_____
_____

DAY 20
Relationships

PRAY through today's Scripture. Use the space below to write a specific prayer for your daughter.

WRITE one item of thankfulness about your daughter on Day 30.

Notes, thoughts, praise...

Relationships

DAY 21

Friends can be a precious gift who help us follow Jesus, or they can be a detriment who draw us away from the Lord. Pray for your daughter's friends to be the life-giving, Jesus-encouraging kind, who point her heart toward the Lord. Also, pray that she would be that kind of friend to her companions.

> ~ Whoever **walks with the wise becomes wise**, but the **companion of fools will suffer harm**. (Proverbs 13:20)
> ~ So you will **walk in the way of the good** and **keep to the paths of the righteous**. (Proverbs 2:20)
> ~ I am a **companion of all who fear you**, **of those who keep your precepts**. (Psalm 119:63)
> ~ And let us consider how to **stir up one another to love and good works**, (Hebrews 10:24)

Jesus, I ask You to help my girl:

~ have wise friends who love and obey You.

_____
_____
_____
_____

~ stay away from foolish friends and the harm that will come from their ideas or activities.

_____
_____
_____
_____

DAY 21
Relationships

~ stay on a good path, following You. And please help me be a good example and companion along the way.

_____
_____
_____
_____

~ keep on Your path, even when the world offers her a tempting alternative.

_____
_____
_____
_____

~ cultivate deep friendships with girls who love You, obey You, and love Your Word.

_____
_____
_____
_____

~ stir others up to love You, and allow her to have companions in her friends and family that cause her to serve You more.

_____
_____
_____
_____

DAY 21
Relationships

In what areas do I see that my daughter has victory with the people in her life?

_____
_____
_____
_____
_____
_____
_____
_____
_____
_____

What specific needs have been revealed after praying for my daughter's relationships?

_____
_____
_____
_____
_____
_____
_____
_____
_____
_____

DAY 21
Relationships

PRAY through today's Scripture. Use the space below to write a specific prayer for your daughter.

WRITE one item of thankfulness about your daughter on Day 30.

Notes, thoughts, praise...

Personality

Personality

DAY 22

As females grow up, they often compare themselves to others and feel dissatisfied with who they are. But your daughter's personality is a gift from the Lord to allow her to complete the work He has for her. For the next four days you will be praying for her own understanding and acceptance of the person God created her to be.

> And he said to me, "**You are my servant**, Israel, **in whom I will be glorified**." ... And now the LORD says, he who **formed me from the womb** to **be his servant**, to bring Jacob back to him; and that Israel might be gathered to him-- for **I am honored in the eyes of the LORD**, and my **God has become my strength**-- (Isaiah 49:3, 5)

Lord, please help my daughter understand:

~ that she is designed perfectly to serve You in the ways You have designed her to.

_____
_____
_____

~ that You can glorify Yourself in the person You created her to be.

_____
_____
_____

DAY 22
Personality

~ that You formed her perfectly from the moment of conception.

_____
_____
_____
_____

~ she has a job of service to do for You.

_____
_____
_____
_____

~ in Your eyes she is perfectly formed, as she is, to bring You honor and to be honored by You.

_____
_____
_____
_____

~ she doesn't have to be strong enough in herself to do what You created her for, but that she must get her strength from You.

_____
_____
_____
_____

DAY 22
Personality

What areas of my daughter's personality are growing and thriving?

_____
_____
_____
_____
_____
_____
_____
_____
_____
_____

What burdens am I carrying about my daughter's personality that I need to give back to Jesus?

_____
_____
_____
_____
_____
_____
_____
_____
_____
_____

DAY 22
Personality

PRAY through today's Scripture. Use the space below to write a specific prayer for your daughter.

_____
_____
_____
_____
_____
_____
_____
_____

WRITE one item of thankfulness about your daughter on Day 30.

Notes, thoughts, praise...

_____
_____
_____
_____
_____
_____
_____
_____
_____

Personality

DAY 23

Your daughter is beautifully designed for her calling as a daughter of the King. Pray today for her to find and walk out that assignment through the power of the Spirit and the strength of Jesus.

> for God **gave us a spirit not of fear** but **of power and love and self-control**. Therefore **do not be ashamed of the testimony about our Lord**, nor of me his prisoner, but **share in suffering for the gospel** by the power of God, who saved us and **called us to a holy calling**, not because of our works but **because of his own purpose and grace**, which he **gave us in Christ Jesus before the ages began**, (2 Timothy 1:7-9)

Creator God, please cause my daughter:

~ to not give in to her fears and help her see that her fear does not come from You.

_____
_____
_____
_____

~ to walk in Your power, serve with Your love, and live in You self-control.

_____
_____
_____
_____

DAY 23
Personality

~ to confidently proclaim her testimony of Your love through her unique personality.

_____
_____
_____
_____

~ to minister to those who are suffering, through whatever means You provide, and help her see the unique ways she is designed to help others.

_____
_____
_____
_____

~ to find her calling.

_____
_____
_____
_____

~ to see Your purpose and grace for her life that You have given her in Jesus.

_____
_____
_____
_____

DAY 23
Personality

What parts of my daughter's personality are a challenge?

_____
_____
_____
_____
_____
_____
_____
_____
_____

How can I praise my daughter about God's design of her personality? (If nothing specific comes to mind then don't forget to ask the Lord for help with an idea.)

_____
_____
_____
_____
_____
_____
_____
_____

DAY 23
Personality

PRAY through today's Scripture. Use the space below to write a specific prayer for your daughter.

WRITE one item of thankfulness about your daughter on Day 30.

Notes, thoughts, praise...

Personality

DAY 24

Since the world tells our girls their value is in how they look, and that their beauty is in what they wear, we need to counter that false message. Pray today for a deep spiritual understanding in your girl of her true worth as a specifically designed girl, who was formed and is loved by her Heavenly Father.

> ~ **Do not let your adorning be external**--the braiding of hair and the putting on of gold jewelry, or the clothing you wear-- but **let your adorning be the hidden person of the heart** with the **imperishable beauty** of a **gentle and quiet spirit**, which in God's sight is very precious. (1 Peter 3:3-4)
>
> ~ Behold, you **delight in truth in the inward being**, and you **teach me wisdom in the secret heart**. (Psalm 51:6)

I ask You Lord to please:

~ help my daughter value what is on her inside more than what is on her outside.

_____
_____
_____
_____

~ help the hidden person of my daughter's heart – the girl You created her to be – grow and develop to the woman You desire her to be.

_____
_____
_____
_____

DAY 24
Personality

~ grow the realization in my daughter of her true beauty that will not fade or change.

~ develop the gentle and quiet spirit in my girl that You desire, but also help her understand what that looks like for her and her personality, which can be different than it looks in others.

~ grow Your truth in the deepest, inner rooms of her heart.

~ teach her Your wisdom in her secret heart.

DAY 24
Personality

Where do I see my daughter struggling with being who God designed her to be?

___

What is something I can do with or for my daughter to encourage her in how she is designed?

___

DAY 22
Personality

PRAY through today's Scripture. Use the space below to write a specific prayer for your daughter.

_____
_____
_____
_____
_____
_____
_____
_____

WRITE one item of thankfulness about your daughter on Day 30.

Notes, thoughts, praise...

_____
_____
_____
_____
_____
_____
_____
_____
_____

Personality

DAY 25

Pray today for your girl's heart as she faces the inevitable struggles and challenges of growing and maturing. You can ask Jesus to give her an eternal understanding that puts today's problems into perspective.

> So **we do not lose heart**. Though our outer self is wasting away, **our inner self is being renewed** day by day. For this **light momentary affliction** is **preparing for us an eternal weight of glory** beyond all comparison, as we look not to the things that are seen but to the things that are unseen. For the **things that are seen are transient**, but the **things that are unseen are eternal**. (2 Corinthians 4:16-18)

Jesus, I ask You to help my girl:

~ not lose heart.

_____
_____
_____
_____

~ by renewing her inner self- the girl she truly is.

_____
_____
_____
_____

DAY 25
Personality

~ move through whatever challenges and struggles she is or will be facing as she matures into a woman.

_____
_____
_____
_____

~ have a vision beyond what is happening now and to see what You are preparing in her future.

_____
_____
_____
_____

~ understand how temporary her struggles are so she can live with joy and hope.

_____
_____
_____
_____

~ gain a peek into the eternal workings of Your plans for her.

_____
_____
_____
_____

DAY 25
Personality

Where does my daughter walk victoriously in understanding her personality to be part of God's design?

_____
_____
_____
_____
_____
_____
_____
_____
_____

What specific needs have been revealed after praying for my daughter's personality?

_____
_____
_____
_____
_____
_____
_____
_____
_____

DAY 25
Personality

PRAY through today's Scripture. Use the space below to write a specific prayer for your daughter.

WRITE one item of thankfulness about your daughter on Day 30.

Notes, thoughts, praise...

Path

Path

DAY 26

The last section of this prayer journal concentrates on praying for your daughter's path. She is designed for a purpose and a job which her enemy would really like to keep her from completing. So, it's vital to pray for her vision, understanding, and courage to follow the Lord.

> "**Before I formed you** in the womb **I knew you**, and **before you were born I consecrated you**; **I appointed you** a prophet to the nations." Then I said, "Ah, Lord GOD! Behold, **I do not know how to speak, for I am only a youth**." But the LORD said to me, "Do not say, 'I am only a youth'; for to **all to whom I send you, you shall go**, and **whatever I command you, you shall speak**. (Jeremiah 1:5-7)

Jesus, I pray that:

~ my daughter would understand she was formed by You for Your purpose.

_____
_____
_____
_____

~ she would rest her future in Your all-knowing hands.

_____
_____
_____
_____

DAY 26
Path

~ she would walk in the path You have consecrated for her.

_____
_____
_____
_____

~ she would be prepared for the job You have appointed her to do.

_____
_____
_____
_____

~ You would give my daughter, as a youth, the courage to act on whatever You call her to do, without excuses.

_____
_____
_____
_____

~ You would help her go wherever You send her, and speak to whomever You command her.

_____
_____
_____
_____

DAY 26
Path

In what ways is my daughter following the Lord as she looks for her path in life?

_____
_____
_____
_____
_____
_____
_____
_____
_____
_____

What burdens am I carrying about my daughter's direction that I need to give back to Jesus?

_____
_____
_____
_____
_____
_____
_____
_____
_____
_____

DAY 26
Path

PRAY through today's Scripture. Use the space below to write a specific prayer for your daughter.

_____
_____
_____
_____
_____
_____
_____
_____

WRITE one item of thankfulness about your daughter on Day 30.

Notes, thoughts, praise...

_____
_____
_____
_____
_____
_____
_____
_____

Path

DAY 27

Options surround our girls for roads to explore and adventures to take. Pray that your daughter will walk lovingly and carefully, and stay on the path the Lord has planned for her. Jesus can be her greatest adventure and most exciting path.

> And **walk in love**, as Christ loved us and gave himself up for us, **a fragrant offering and sacrifice** to God. ... **Look carefully then how you walk**, **not as unwise but as wise**, **making the best use of the time**, because the days are evil. Therefore do not be foolish, but **understand what the will of the Lord is**. (Ephesians 5:2, 15-17)

Father God, I ask You:

~ to please show my daughter how to walk the path You have for her in love and in a way that honors You.

_____
_____
_____
_____

~ to teach her how to live her life as an offering and sacrifice to You.

_____
_____
_____
_____

DAY 27
Path

~ to give her the wisdom to look carefully at the choices she is making and where she is walking.

~ to please shower wisdom and understanding on her.

~ to help her use her time well and fruitfully.

~ to assist her in seeing, understanding, and walking in Your will.

DAY 27
Path

When is it a challenge for my daughter to understand the way she should go?

How can I praise my daughter about the path she is on? (If nothing specific comes to mind then don't forget to ask the Lord for help with an idea.)

DAY 27
Path

PRAY through today's Scripture. Use the space below to write a specific prayer for your daughter.

WRITE one item of thankfulness about your daughter on Day 30.

Notes, thoughts, praise...

Path

DAY 28

Trusting the Lord when the future is uncertain challenges adults, much less young women. Pray today for your girl to understand the faithfulness of the Lord to lead and protect her, as she follows Him, even when her way seems unclear.

> The **steps of a man are established by the LORD**, when **he delights in his way**; though **he fall, he shall not be cast headlong**, for the **LORD upholds his hand**. I have been young, and now am old, yet I have not seen the righteous forsaken or his children begging for bread. **He is ever lending generously**, and **his children become a blessing**. (Psalm 37:23-26)

Lord, please help my daughter understand:

~ that her steps are established by You in love.

_____
_____
_____
_____

~ she can delight in the way You have for her as You delight in her.

_____
_____
_____
_____

DAY 28
Path

~ that even when she falls, she will not be abandoned by You.

~ she can rest her hand in Yours and let You lead the way.

~ she can trust You to supply her every need along the way.

~ the privilege she has of being a blessing wherever she goes.

DAY 28
Path

Where do I see my daughter struggling with seeing and/or following the path God has for her?

_____
_____
_____
_____
_____
_____
_____
_____
_____

What is something I can do with or for my daughter to encourage her in the direction she is going? How can I demonstrate my love for her, no matter where she is right now?

_____
_____
_____
_____
_____
_____
_____
_____
_____

DAY 28
Path

PRAY through today's Scripture. Use the space below to write a specific prayer for your daughter.

WRITE one item of thankfulness about your daughter on Day 30.

Notes, thoughts, praise...

Path

DAY 29

Uncertainty of the right way makes following a challenge. Today, you are praying that your daughter will see the Lord and hear His voice so that she can stay on His path, even during difficult times.

> …He will surely be gracious to you at the sound of your cry. As **soon as he hears it, he answers you**. And though the Lord give you the **bread of adversity** and the water of affliction, yet your Teacher will not hide himself anymore, but **your eyes shall see your Teacher**. And **your ears shall hear a word behind you**, saying, "**This is the way, walk in it**," when you **turn to the right or when you turn to the left**. (Isaiah 30:19b-21)

Dear Lord, as my daughter searches for her path, please:

~ help her confidently call on You with any of her questions.

_____
_____
_____
_____

~ keep her from becoming discouraged at the difficult obstacles that will surely come.

_____
_____
_____
_____

DAY 29
Path

~ cause my daughter to see You so she can learn from You all she needs to know.

_____
_____
_____
_____

~ open her ears so that she can hear Your still, small voice.

_____
_____
_____
_____

~ help her see and hear Your leading in the way she should walk.

_____
_____
_____
_____

~ direct her to make the changes she needs to stay on Your path.

_____
_____
_____
_____

DAY 29
Path

In what ways do I see my daughter developing into who God has designed her to be?

_____
_____
_____
_____
_____
_____
_____
_____
_____

What specific needs have been revealed after praying for my daughter's path?

_____
_____
_____
_____
_____
_____
_____
_____
_____

DAY 29
Path

PRAY through today's Scripture. Use the space below to write a specific prayer for your daughter.

WRITE one item of thankfulness about your daughter on Day 30.

Notes, thoughts, praise...

Thankful

Thanksgiving

DAY 30

Today you will rejoice and praise the Lord for the girl He created Your daughter to be. No matter what is happening in her life, thanking the Lord wields a mighty weapon over her. Praise the Lord for each item you recorded over the past 29 days. Don't be discouraged, be grateful. Always.

> **I thank my God in all my remembrance of you**, always in every prayer of mine for you all making my prayer with joy, (Philippians 1:3-4)
>
> **Rejoice in the Lord always**; again I will say, rejoice. ... do not be anxious about anything, but in everything **by prayer and supplication with thanksgiving let your requests be made known to God**. And the peace of God, which surpasses all understanding, will guard your hearts and your minds in Christ Jesus. (Philippians 4:4, 6-7)

Thank You, Lord, for the girl You created my daughter to be.

_____
_____
_____
_____

I choose to rejoice in You, Lord, and promise to pray for anything that concerns me. I choose to pray instead of worry.

_____
_____
_____
_____

Thank the Lord for all the following items:

Day 1 _____

Day 2 _____

Day 3 _____

Day 4 _____

Day 5 _____

Day 6 _____

Day 7 _____

Day 8 _____

Day 9 _____

Day 10 _____

I give thanks to my God always for you because of the grace of God that was given you in Christ Jesus (1 Corinthians 1:4)

Day 11

Day 12

Day 13

Day 14

Day 15

Day 16

Day 17

Day 18

Day 19

Day 20

I do not cease to give thanks for you,
remembering you in my prayers (Ephesians 1:16)

Day 21 _____

Day 22 _____

Day 23 _____

Day 24 _____

Day 25 _____

Day 26 _____

Day 27 _____

Day 28 _____

Day 29 _____

Day 30 _____

I will give thanks to the LORD with my whole heart; I will recount all of your wonderful deeds. (Psalm 9:1 ESV)

Keep Praying!

Keep Praying! DAY 31

Yahoo! You have completed this prayer journal. I am so proud of you. But the next question is: what are you going to pray for next? Your praying assignment never ends, not as long as you have breath. So keep praying! You can go back through this journal again. It is designed to be used over and over. Or you can use another aide. But you can also pray through any verse in the Bible for your girl. Praying for her is the MOST powerful influence you have in her life. Never stop. Keep praying.

> "…**I give myself to prayer**." (Psalm 109:4b)
>
> **I love the LORD**, because he has heard my voice and **my pleas for mercy**. Because **he inclined his ear to me**, therefore **I will call on him as long as I live**. (Psalm 116:1-2)
>
> May our sons in their youth be like plants full grown, **our daughters like corner pillars** cut for the structure of a palace (Psalm 144:12)

Dear Jesus, I ask You to:

~ help me to stay committed to praying

_____
_____
_____
_____

~ help me love You even more.

_____
_____
_____
_____

DAY 31
Keep Praying

~ have mercy on me and on my daughter.

~ continue to incline Your ear to me. Thank You for Your nearness and Your listening.

~ help me not grow weary so that I will continue to call on You for my daughter as long as You give me breath.

~ continue to form and shape my daughter to be a strong pillar that builds and supports Your Kingdom and declares Your truth.

DAY 31
Keep Praying!

What has God revealed to me in the past 30 days that has encouraged my prayer life?

_____
_____
_____
_____
_____
_____
_____
_____
_____

What specific items am I convicted to continue in prayer for my daughter in the future? (After you write them here, you might want to post them in a visible location so you will be reminded to **Keep Praying!**)

_____
_____
_____
_____
_____
_____
_____
_____

DAY 31
Keep Praying!

Use the space below to write a prayer of thanksgiving to God for your daughter, including the specific ways He created and formed her.

___

Rejoice always, pray without ceasing,
give thanks in all circumstances;
for this is the will of God in Christ Jesus for you.
(1 Thessalonians 5:16-18)

Great job, good and faithful servant! Your prayer matters and will deeply affect your daughter. Congratulations on completing this journal. Now go forward and keep praying!

Resources

Resources

Prayer Needs

Resources

Prayer Needs

Resources

Prayer Needs

Resources

Prayer Needs

Daughter Questionnaire

Daughter's name: _____
_____

Describe your daughter's relationship with the Lord:
_____
_____
_____
_____

Describe your daughter's personality:
_____
_____
_____
_____

What are the biggest challenges facing your daughter:
_____
_____
_____
_____

What are your daughter's greatest strengths:
_____
_____
_____
_____

Daughter Questionnaire

Daughter's name: _____

Describe your daughter's relationship with the Lord:
_____
_____
_____
_____

Describe your daughter's personality:
_____
_____
_____
_____

What are the biggest challenges facing your daughter:
_____
_____
_____
_____

What are your daughter's greatest strengths:
_____
_____
_____
_____

Daughter Questionnaire

Daughter's name: _____

Describe your daughter's relationship with the Lord:

_____
_____
_____

Describe your daughter's personality:

_____
_____
_____

What are the biggest challenges facing your daughter:

_____
_____
_____

What are your daughter's greatest strengths:

_____
_____
_____

Daughter Questionnaire

Daughter's name: _____

Describe your daughter's relationship with the Lord:
_____
_____
_____

Describe your daughter's personality:
_____
_____
_____

What are the biggest challenges facing your daughter:
_____
_____
_____

What are your daughter's greatest strengths:
_____
_____
_____

For more prayer help read Susan's book:

Unceasing:
A Parent's Guide To
Conquer Worry And Pray With
Power

Available on Amazon

Susan Macias is a writer and speaker who uses truth, humor, and insight to encourage women. Understanding the battle of weariness and discouragement that ladies face, she writes and speaks to build up women so they can faithfully follow Jesus, serve their families, and build the Kingdom.

Susan's book, *UNCEASING: A Parent's Guide To Conquer Worry And Pray With Power* is available on Amazon. Married to her college sweetheart for thirty-three years, Nathan and Susan have raised seven children. She adores her role as "Daisy" to her three granddaughters.

For more information or to contact Susan visit:
www.susankmacias.com

Read her blog	Hear or ask her to speak	Interact on social media

Facebook: Susan K Macias
Instagram: Susan K Macias
Twitter: @SusanKMacias
YouTube: Susan Macias

Made in the USA
Columbia, SC
22 July 2021